Young Poets - North of England

Anthology 2021-2022

ISBN: 9798838353207
Imprint: Independently published

ACKNOWLEDGEMENTS

The National Literacy Trust would like to thank all our partner venues: The Bronte Parsonage Museum, Blackpool Central Library, St George's Hall, and Bradford Industrial Museum for welcoming students and providing such a memorable and enriching experience.

Thanks as well to the educators in the classroom and in our partner cultural venues. Thanks to the poets Toria Garbutt, Kirsty Taylor, Matt Abbott, Charlotte Wetton, Ant Briscoe, and Nabeela Ahmed, who helped shape the students' work, and of course, to the students for their hard work and dedication.

And last but not least, thank you to our wonderful funders, the Paul Hamlyn Foundation. Without their generous support, this project would not have been possible.

CONTENTS

INTRODUCTION

This year's Young Poets programmes in Bradford and Blackpool continued to be affected by the COVID-19 pandemic. It is therefore a testament to the dedication of the educators, poets, and pupils who took part that this anthology exists.

We also led a multilingual strand of the Young Poets programme as part of this year's project, to encourage pupils and teachers to share their home languages or dialects in class. The number of pupils who chose to do so and the quality of their poetry appears to justify our decision to go ahead with this.

The poems here range from explorations of identity and language, to considerations of big ideas such as freedom and belonging.

Pupils demonstrate that no matter our age or experience, poetry allows us to think about and explore these ideas. They have shown that in difficult times, poetry can help us to learn about ourselves and provide a compass to navigate our way in the world.

KINCRAIG PRIMARY - BLACKPOOL

Freedom

In the window of freedom...

Explore and adore the nature around you.

In the window of freedom...

A new beginning is waiting for you.

In the window of freedom...

A butterfly spreads its wings and rises high.

In the window of freedom...

A new fresh life like a beautiful rose beginning to grow.

In the window of freedom...

A continuous journey just for you.

Chelsey

Aspire

In the window of aspire...

The sun shines through,

like a bright, beaming light.

In the window of aspire...

The face of a person,

ready to achieve their goals.

In the window of aspire...

You are filled with hope,

inspired for a better future.

In the window of aspire...

The red light shining on the target,

you are heading where you want to be.

In the window of aspire...

Make a plan and reach high,

to the sky and above the clouds.

Elsie

Belong

In the window of belong...

There is a family together,

like a perfect jigsaw puzzle.

In the window of belong...

There is someone safe,

having a wonderful time with their family.

In the window of belong...

You join a new group,

feeling excited and cool.

In the window of belong...

A happy house,

feeling excited for the future.

                                                        Joshua

Imagine

In the window of imagine...

Let your mind be free,

explore every space.

In the window of imagine...

Create a new world,

full of excitement and joy.

In the window of imagine ...

Invent more creations,

build your ideas.

In the window of imagine...

Dream big dreams,

you can achieve.

Lucas

Freedom

In the window of freedom…

You have the liberty,

live a happy life.

In the window of freedom…

Your wings are set free,

travel wherever you want to be.

In the window of freedom…

People roam freely,

happily going wherever they please.

In the window of freedom…

People are free,

to do and say whatever they please.

In the window of freedom..

You are resilient,

free from any stress.

Noah

APPLETON ACADEMY - BRADFORD

Rugby Life

When I start mi heart starts racing,

As I get ready to catch t' ball.

My hands get into position

Legs fired t' go.

I start belting through all t' players,

I run one hundred miles an hour

And I score!

Jamie

A Trip to Blackpool

My favourite place is Blackpool,

Eternal fun.

Relaxing sea and sand on never-ending beaches.

Wet and crazy rides in the funfair,

Donkey rides and rock.

Calm and relaxing sitting in the sun,

Blackpool - a place for everyone.

Kadie

Lines of Morning

When I wake up,

Bright light from the bulb overhead

Shines in my hazel brown eyes.

When I wake up,

All my negative thoughts are left behind.

When I wake up,

I see the bright orange sky,

A vibrant yellow sun shining.

A new day is dawning,

That's my morning.

Codie- Louise

The Beauty of Running

Running is freedom,

You never forget how to run.

People run because it lets them feel good,

I feel myself when I run.

Fresh air pushing into my face,

Pain streaming into my legs.

Long, middle or short distance,

Any element of athletics.

Running makes me sweat,

Wind blowing in my hair.

I wish everyone could see the beauty of running.

Eva

The Sea

The sea is a wonderful place,

Each one being different.

A wonderful sight when two seas meet,

Can't be beaten.

The sea can be calm,

Can be very quiet.

With only the sound of dolphins diving.

All you can see is waves scudding by,

Nothing can beat the sea.

Under the sea are plants,

Coral and seaweed.

The only unwelcome event

Is seaweed in my mouth.

Some things can beat the sea.

Freya

FARFIELD PRIMARY - BRADFORD

An Horrible Life

All of the machines

CLASHING, BANGING

All over

Every second

Kids getting no breaks

Every morning

Every night

Just the same

People getting sick

Drinking the perilous water

What a horrible life to have!

Ethan

The Machines

The machines are crashing

The machines are screeching

The machines are as loud as dinosaurs

The children are in danger

The machines are hundreds of lions roaring

The machines are musty

The machines are very dirty

The children feel sick

The buildings are huge

The whole place is perilous

It's not fair

Aaqif

They'll Get Punished

Clashing, banging, screeching machines

Children picking up scraps of wool

If they don't do the job right

They'll get punished

Every day

Every minute

The manager comes in and punishes everyone

And says get down

Scrub those floors until they're polished

What a horrible life they had!

Rhiannon

I Saw

I saw old vehicles

I saw old trains

I saw number plates on the walls

Jowett, old fashioned, remarkable

I saw machines moving

I saw wool pulling

I saw wheels turning

Vibrations, clashing, cranking

I saw different bedrooms

I saw vivid colours

I saw various buildings

Huge, interesting patterns

This was my fun time at the Bradford Industrial Museum

Ronnie

My Past Life of Terror

Our life, our life, this is our life

The noises were horror

The fright they had

It was like light would never strike

The monster that hurt me

Is this our legacy?

Our community?

Stepping through life future and past

It was a surprise to see us like this right now

2022 is a bolt of life

1840 was a shrivel of might

It would never stop

Like thunder would always strike under

The valley we had as the mills would grow like thousands of flowers

blooming

Our life, our life, this is our life

Lexi

If I Were a Child Working in the Mill

BANG, BASH, BOOM, BUZZ!

The machines would be screeching at the top of their lungs

Ah noisy!

PING, SMASH, BANG, CRASH!

A window crashed in the maid's room

She screamed

Pulled into the attic

And never seen again

Where did she go? Nobody knows

What happened to her? Nobody knows

Layla-Mae

Nellie, Nellie, Nellie

Nellie, Nellie, Nellie, she's a masterpiece

But now she's retired

Nellie, Nellie, Nellie, she's as large as a house

But she needs a good clean

Nellie, Nellie, Nellie, she's 100 years old

But still she's going

Nellie, Nellie, Nellie, she made me feel amazed

And she should be very proud!

Jacob

Bradford Industrial Museum

I was fascinated

The classroom was as frightening as the devil

The machines were as deafening as bombs

The trains were shining like butterflies

But the most unforgettable part was

Nellie, Nellie, Nellie

The finest train in Bradford!

Jack

Bradford's Industrial Museum

It's a great place

There's plenty of space

Everything's old

And nothing's been sold

But the best thing was

The big, big cold coat

Its houses are tattered

And they look battered

 Everything's fixed

And no poles look like sticks

But the best thing was

The super, super sensible stable

Jaycie

Bradford's Past, Present and Future

I heard the screaming
I saw a pig running
I could taste mouldy bread
I touched the loud machines
I could smell the dust in the air

Bradford is a big shopping centre
Bradford is Willy Wonka's store room
Bradford is a wine cellar
Bradford is a bubbling pan
Bradford is a giant shoe

Quick, sprinting, flying cars
Flying, big, speeding hover boards
Charging, powering, electronic bodies
Magic comes to life.
By Melody M
The Industrial Museum
I felt fascinated
Never been here before

The printing was magnificent
How did they make that way back then?

I hated the machinery noise

My ears were shaking and exploding

The waterwheel was impressive

How did they use these?

But the best thing was Nellie

The engine was as enormous as an elephant

Hussnain

The Old Museum

The old water wheel

The old machines

The old houses

We wandered around the museum

The old train

The old chair

The old cars

We saw them all

Ruby

CO-OP ACADEMY THE GRANGE - BRADFORD

The Arcade

The arcade is more than a dot on a map.

I love the arcade

because that's where *piyaj* and *maza* is made.

The arcade is very bright

Full of different *rangeen* lights.

The lights are like the stars in Pakistan,

where you sit on a *sabz* grassy field on some random land,

and where you see the full bright moon,

and the *chandi* replaces the lights on the street.

The arcade is where you can hear *hansi* and talking,

You're with your friends and family, and not

Alone,

which makes this beautiful *donya* fun.

Arzoo

My Room

My bedroom is more than just a room.

It's home.

My bedroom can be as relaxing as a sauna,

sometimes it's as crazy as a zoo.

Me and *pishou* chilling on my bed,

with the LED lights on the colour red.

My *kabala* hugs me on the coldest nights,

while I'm looking out the window staring at the stars which shine bright.

The streets roar on freezing nights,

I feel at ease knowing I'm in my bedroom tonight.

My bedroom is more than just a room.

It's my safe place.

Aleeza

My Home

My home is more than a dot on the map.

My home frees me,

My home eases me,

My home relaxes me.

Every meal I take,

all the spices,

Masalas and

Flavours each bringing

back a *garma* and nostalgic

core memory.

My living room fills with light,

even on the darkest of nights.

My home keeps me safe.

It covers me like a *kabala,*

just like the stars cover the night sky.

The clouds cover the sky,

the ocean waves cover the land.

My home is *my* place.

It is definitely more than a dot on a map.

Zara

My Auntie's House

My Auntie's house is more than a dot on a map.

It's a place of freedom.

It is a peaceful sea of tranquillity.

I feel like the house speaks to me.

Hamza

Bradford

Bradford is more than you can see in sight,

with extravagant entertainment and gloomy lights.

A visit to Braford can be explained as critical,

But no need to worry as you won't have to be sceptical.

The streets of Bradford are where I roam,

I am more than happy to call Bradford my home.

Binyameen

Moldova

Moldova is not just a dot on a map,

it's a place where your thoughts unwrap.

It's a free space,

where everyone feels like they're in outer space.

Moldova mea ie jrumosă,

Moldova mea ie valuroasă.

Aici am crescut,

aici mam născut.

The sweet apple bite,

and the bright stars waiting for night.

The ice creams are minging,

and all the kids are swinging.

All my thoughts are with Moldova,

being there feels like being in nova.

Sunte multe tării pe lume dragi.

Dar ţara mea îmi este cel mai drag.

Vanessa

My Sister's House

My sister's house is bigger than a dot on the world's map.

My sister's house is big

My sister's house is fun

My sister's house makes me *khush*

My sister's house is a place where I feel proud

My sister's house contains two boys that are loud.

My nephews make me a proud uncle

My nephews are playing with the carpet, roaring

My nephews' toys make me laugh

My nephews' food sing to them to eat

My nephews are as naughty as horses

My nephews are clever

My nephews are always laughing and enjoying life.

My sister's house is bigger than a dot on the world's map.

My sister's house is a place where I feel loved.

Dil Shaan

My Mosque

A mosque is more than a dot on a map.

This is my mosque.

A place like no other,

A place I love...dearly.

It's quiet, peaceful, relaxing

and filled with beautiful recitation.

This is my mosque.

This is my religion.

Mostapha

Slovakia

Slovakia is more than a dot on a map,

Christmas in Slovakia

Seeing your family

The smell of the amazing food

The thick snow is falling and little children on *sanky*.

Gold, sparkle, *cigane*

Christmas is here

The dads cooking *svine*

The mums decorating the house with bright *svetla*

The traditional food you can smell all around

The traditional dances with the girls and boys

The kind people always giving to the poor

So a traditional Christmas is a beautiful Christmas

Slovakia is more than a dot on a map; it's a home

Not just to me

But also the hard working *cigane*

Jesika

Turkey

Turkey is more than a dot on a map

Istanbul is pretty, calming, it's like home for me.

Bursa is pretty as well

If I get a chance, I would love to go to Bursa to meet the Boran family

such as *Istanbulli menyazon*, then after I would go to Istanbul to listen

to the amazing songs and *latany emeberek dancony aszenire*.

I see kids running around to get food,

But can I tell you a secret, Istanbul food is good but not better than my

mom's *guasleves* with some pepper on it as seasoning.

The thing I love the most about Istanbul is the view.

The view will shock you - it's amazing.

The view shining in your eyes and taking my breath away

With the charming and amazing styles people have.

The weather is beautiful, when it's nice.

There's music in the street and it makes me feel *nugot*,

And walking past the big buildings makes me feel like I am in a dream!

Amazing beautiful cars and clothes

It is the time for Eid! The music is dancing in my ears

With excitement it is amazing seeing smiles on children while filling

their pockets with *pesay*.

Jesika D

Pakistan

Pakistan is more than a dot on a map
It is a place to relax, has freedom
It is a gift from God.

The smell of the *garam* food is mesmerising
When you first see the food,
It makes you want to eat more of it
All of it.

The taste of the *tandaa paani*
Is a gift from God.
When you first drink it
You get pumped with enough energy

The fresh *garmi* weather
Is a place to relax and enjoy
The fresh air when you first smell it
Will get it in your head.

The wild animals: *bakriya, kangrood, zarafah*
Are tall and friendly when you pet them
they will become your *dost*.

Eid is a peaceful and charming day
It is a day for *mazaa*

With your *dost* and cousins and *chacha*

Pockets will be filled up with *pesay*

Ami's aunties, sisters, cousins doing *mehndi*.

Shaadi is different from English weddings

Gana, Gadiyan and fireworks

Kids will be munching candy floss

Taunting their parents to give them more.

Zain

Saudi Arabia

Saudi Arabia is more than just a dot on the map
It is bright and majestic
It is not just a country
It's a second home for me.

The aroma of the food attracts me
Pakora, kebab, samosa
The beautiful shape of the *samosa* and *pakora*
With a mouth-watering taste to it.

The heat of the *garam* sun
Gleaming down at me, making me feel golden
The sight of the majestic moon in the evening sky
The busy streets and the calming air.

Everyone rushing to *namaaz*
Wearing beautiful clothes
Listening to the *azaan*
It's time to pray.

Meraaj

A Welcoming Country

Turkey is more than a simple dot on the map
It's a welcoming country
The doors are always wide open, everyone is calm
The *paani* was bright blue and clear.

The whole country is beautiful and bright
The journey is tiring but it was worth the wait
This is only once in a lifetime,
I hope to go back soon.

Eid is after the holy month of Ramadan
On Eid, it is *bohot garmi*, spending time with family
Garmi, mouth-watering food like Samosa, Shawarma
Seekh kebab, the fresh *tanda paani* dripping down my mouth
Everyone has bright smiles, giving *salaam* to each other.

Muntazir

Where I Am at peace

Pakistan is more than a dot on a map

It is a place of power and freedom

It is where I am at peace

As the blue river flows gently down the stream,

People are splashing away, taking off the heat

I jump in... my cousins with me

The best thing about this for me is being together with them.

Walking through bazaar, I see my favourite shop

The karai gosht was calling out for me!

While the smell melts my nose, my mum looked at me

I had a wide grin on my face.

The shaadis are a different mazaa here

As the bride and groom walk down the hall

I can hear people playing the dhol as the golay shoot up

People dancing knowing it is a gift for them

And a celebration for others.

Umar

TONG LEADERSHIP ACADEMY - BRADFORD

Be Yourself!

Be kind like helping nurses treat their patients.

Explore through new things like every day is a new adventure.

You own inspiration, like a box of ideas.

Open your mind like it's a hidden door leading towards imagination.

Unpredicted turns will come your way like a winning lottery ticket landing on your lap.

Reach for the stars as if they are like an inch away.

Speak out to haters and drown their voices in happy memories.

Expect sudden changes as if you're walking into a new dimension of dinosaurs.

Let your dreams run free like a dandelion ascending through the air.

Find your true self that hides beneath somebody else.

Ruby

The World is in Flames!

Burning, screaming help me now, killers, pollution

What can we do?

People killing, kidnapping, poison, everywhere we go there is

racism, murders, disease taking out little ones,

COVID, flu.

What can we do?

Pollution taking over the world, cars, factories, trains and planes.

What can we do?

Animals dying, ice melting, climate change is killing our planet.

Fire is breaking the homes of our animals.

Floods, tsunamis, earthquakes are getting worse. Tragedy

Happening everywhere. We are infecting our planet.

What can we do?

Paper and plastic is killing our planet.

Paper is from our trees. Why are we killing our trees?

Plastic choking our turtles.

Save us. Save us.

What can we do?

Ellie-Marie

Believe in Yourself!

Believe in yourself. Believe!

Have confidence.

Don't let the worries creep up on you

Then strangle yourself in the dark.

The anxiety of not knowing what's

going to happen in the next

Minute, hour, month, year.

Keep calm and believe.

Let the stress fade away.

PUT YOURSELF FORWARD!

Priscilla

Lose

Anxiety is stressful and I know it can be
Frightful, but don't lose it.

I know it feels like anxiety punches
Your stomach, but don't lose it.

I know it feels like there's someone pouring oil
into your throat, and your brain is becoming foggy,
but don't lose it.

I know it's like your vision is painted with black paint
but don't faint.

I know your mouth sometime tastes
like blood and tears start to flood,
But don't lose it.

Do not stress, everything will be good.

Remember, never lose it.

Nikola

Don't Give Up

Giving up on your dreams feels like giving up all
Hope. Giving up on your dreams looks like you have
Failed yourself. Giving up on your dreams sounds like
You couldn't achieve what you always wanted. Don't
Give up; you will make it.

Don't give up, success is on the line.
In the darkest of times, light will always be ahead.
Follow your dreams as when you succeed,
You will know you have made it,
You will feel joyful and as happy as could be.
Don't give up; you will make it.

No person can go to the heights of Heaven,
If first they don't go to the deepest depths of Hell.
You can do it as long as you stay hopeful,
You will do it.
Don't give up; you will make it.
Don't give up; you will make it.
You will make it.

Tyler

The Seven Seas

Sailing on the salty seas
Dirty sailors and parrots with fleas
The sails are high, the navy we loathe
Searching for the treasure trove.

Sailing on the sickly seas
Full of infections and scurvy in our knees
The stakes are high, enemies inbound
Listen to the ship, the cannonball sound.

Sailing on the wonderful seas
Selling our riches to get the fees
The anchors high, setting sail once more
We all rejoice, the wine we pour.

Sailing on the foggy seas
Most of us regretting our money-filled dreams
We carry on, straight into the unknown
Making sure we get our next loan.

Sailing on the fearsome seas
Spending our time fending of thieves
We never give up, it's etched in our mind
To dream to fight, to dream to find.

Sailing on the tranquil seas

The sun comes up, the light makes us sneeze

Our eyes light up, has our voyage come to a close?

The island is in sight; no more foes.

Sailing on the seven seas

But the treasure chests are locked we need the keys

We raise the sails, fill our cups

We recall our message: never give up!

Jake

Remember

Remember

Those days when you wanted time to stop

When you wanted that moment to never end

Remember

Your goals

Your dreams

Where are they now?

Why did they disappear?

Remember

That feeling

That moment

And don't give up

Remember

That feeling

That dream

And keep going.

Remember

When you thought this feeling would last

That anything would change after you open your eyes

When you though life was like heaven

So why did it change?

Why did you change?

So when you feel like giving up

Remember

That feeling

That slight light of hope you had

And keep going,

Do it

For your younger self

For their dream

Remember

And keep going.

Zara

Stay Strong

When you sit in the dark all alone

The horrors playing in your mind.

Stay Strong.

When they beat you down

No one to help

No one to protect you

Stay Strong.

Your time will come

To turn towards the light

And leave this place

Stay Strong.

When you get pulled from heaven

Dragged through hell

When you open the door

To the world

You will be ready.

Sohan

No Room for Racism

People are from different places
And they all have different faces
They can be black, white or green
But that doesn't mean you can be mean.

Everyone speaks different languages
And they all have different challenges
Some can be rich
While some can be poor
But we are all the same under the law.

We all go to different places for holidays
Like USA, France or Norway
We eat different foods to celebrate festivals
That's why we live in different capitals.

Every person is special.
And we all have different potential
And we all have different abilities
This is what we call DIVERSITY.

Adam

Stay as Yourself

Stay as yourself,

Even if the taste of anxiety burns your throat.

Even if the scent of worry stings your nose.

Stay.

No matter what your culture, background or race,

Stay as yourself.

Don't let your identity erase.

People work like machines,

They all have their ways.

Don't be like them,

Don't go to waste.

Some act like animals,

They can't be tamed.

But even animals have lives,

Don't be enslaved.

Life is short, don't let it go to waste,

But life is also a journey,

Go at your own pace.

You have you own body,

Mind and brain.

Do not let others

Destroy your reign.

You are a queen,

King or ruler.

Make sure you're seen

Or your life will waste sooner.

So stay as yourself,

Don't let others break your pace.

Stay as yourself,

You have one body, don't let it go to waste.

You are not a machine,

Don't fall into their standards.

Stay as yourself,

If we were all the same, life would be a pain.

Stay as yourself.

Karolina

BRONTE GIRLS ACADEMY –

BRADFORD

We Remember

I remember leaving the coach and entering the Bradford Industrial
Museum,

A place filled with stories and history.

It was as if I had walked into the ancient past,

Into this building overflowing with glory.

I remember seeing the rusted nails,

As well as the cars of well-known history.

Giving opportunities of work,

But more so for the unseen poetry.

I viewed the different methods of weaving, spinning, dying,

The printers, vehicles, and foundries.

That helped develop the Industrial Revolution,

The amazing building with limitless boundaries.

I remember when I saw the mass production,

The different workhouses and forms of child labour

That took place during the Industrial Revolution,

Along with the locomotive, Nellie.

Bariya, Maryam, Noor and Isha

Bradford Industrial Museum

As I entered the museum,

Wonder and knowledge bestowed on me.

Old creations going back decades,

Inventions so fascinating you have never seen.

Curiouser and Curiouser, I see a man as old as can be,

He holds a sign, 'Welcome Bronte Girls Academy.'

Up we go first floor, ready to see more,

Machines chugged, turbines cranked and retired trains still steaming.

Staircases and corridors forming corridors a labyrinth unknowingly,

Several floors of ancient artifacts making me wonder and ponder,

A giant train named Nellie was on display,

It is said she was transport in the industrial period of dismay.

Up we go to the mill managers home,

Vintage and exquisite, nothing like you would ever think.

Nothing like the miserable industrial period, clean and elite.

Magnificent and vast, with mysteries that lie in the past.

Fiza, Sadia , Rafya and Aisha

Bradford Industrial Museum

Stepping into the Bradford Industrial Museum,

Many objects bottled up with secrets,

Exploring the wonders around the museum,

My mind was full of curiosity

I absorbed the history,

Filled with mystery,

Weavings and sewings,

All were ancient,

All were mesmerising,

All in an old building.

I stared in awe at the machines of ink,

I was so amazed I could not blink.

Back in time we shall travel,

Secrets we will unravel,

Mysteries soon to be revealed.

Hearing the looms,

Working and weaving of fabric.

I reached up to a coat that stood up so tall and broad.

It was full of culture, background explaining a meaning of its own,

but it was left in the darkness all alone.

Away from the spotlight, there it hung, no attention it brought.

I stood there wondering how it felt, appreciating the moment.

I turned to look around at the clinging and clanging of metal.

People gasped and studied these machines as they roared.

All around me, antiques, now refurbished,

All shining like stars in the sky.

But soon I realised, it was time to say goodbye!

Haleema, Inaya, Hamna and Asma

I remember

I remember arriving the Bradford industrial museum,

Home to mystery and intrigue,

I roam around

Seeking mysterious machines.

Watching the porcelain doll stare into the very depth of my soul,

Making my blood boil,

Odd objects with tied tongues,

They try to speak to me,

From the top of their lungs, but cannot.

I stepped into a room,

Where a coat as big as an elephant,

with intricate designs and cultural messages shone through,

With a spark of light,

Inspiration came flooding though me.

The old cars,

Once driving cobbled streets,

Glorious once,

But now rusty and corroded,

Once as shiny as the twinkling stars at night,

But now as ancient as the Egyptian mummies.

Inayah, Ayesha, Ammara, Hiba and Aminah

Bradford Industrial Museum Poem

I remember stepping through the doors and away from the pouring rain,

into the ancient museum, filled with old things and history.

Further on, we ended up at a factory where metal would be casted and melted - a foundry.

I trudged up the towering staircase and discovered a room full of old cars,

looking like they had been restored from the 80s.

But what caught my eye most, was Nellie, a large, mesmerizing steam engine,

who had an incredibly strong horsepower.

Then we went to the exhibit where clothes were made, I looked up in awe

at a beautiful coat, but then I saw the machines clinging and clanging...

I am just a boring coat hung on the wall that people look at, find it outstanding

and then walk away. I stare enviously opposite me, to see machines that get more

use then me.

Humna, Anaaya and Malkesha

Bradford Industrial Museum

I remember stepping in,

my shoes clacking on the hard concrete,

cars and cars as far as the eye could see,

I wonder how old they could be?

Upstairs machines roared as they weaved for hours,

echoing in halls acting with power,

as we ascended up the spiraling stairs,

the Victorian era starts to flare.

Workhouses, revolution, manual labour,

Looks like history's doing us a favor,

Victorians loved to cherish things,

so we claimed of rust with a secret mist.

Victorians portraits were to finish on

the historical premises, exquisitely done,

realistic of course this is on my

bucket list, for sure!

Scavangers work 20 hours per day,

while other children go

eat, sleep and play.

In the workhouse where they stay

some are orphans, some are stray.

Maryam , Ayza, Aimen and Aminah

I Remember it All...

We started off at the choo-choo trains and the clown-looking cars.

Used to pull fat, lumpy drivers.

Powered by humour!

Let me tell you, child labour was real.

The little clowns had too much on their plates – illegal!

There was a choo-choo train stop

 Fuel powered car stops

And bus stops.

I read a notice which said, 'all drivers must remove their dirty socks and

underwear or miasma will occur.'

I remember

We visited the mechanical printing press

We learned about ink

The coloured mud

A set of numbers and letters.

I remember the Industrial Museum.

We learned a lot.

We really did.

Hafsa, Anzeela, Laila and Kulsoom

Our Visit

Our good old friend Nellie, the locomotive train,

The Blacksmith forging metal objects,

The vintage printing press productions,

The diverse coat of cultures

hung onto the sapphire walls of the factory.

DRIP, DRIP, DRIP!

I can still hear the sounds of the jet-black ink

exploring the different fonts and colours.

it was mesmerising to see.

Wow! The mill manager's house.

The old-fashioned living room,

Inhabited by a lonely ginger fluffy cat.

The detailed stain glass windows,

A variety of colours.

How magnificent!

Saniyah, Sehr and Fatima

The Adventure

I remember, antique atmosphere

Overwhelmed by the shuddering machinery.

It was as if past became present right before our eyes.

With the printing press and the type writer revealed,

It felt like the past was unwinding.

While the Blacksmith forged a nail from the fire, we were in disbelief.

When we watched the ink drip, splatter and dry,

I remember the magic I felt.

This is many years ago.

The life of our ancestors – Our Bradford ancestors.

When we saw the newspaper being printed,

we re-imagined history before our twinkling eyes.

Hibbah, Aimen, Abeeha, Inayah and Innayah

Industrial Revolution

I remember seeing the beginning of the Industrial Revolution:

Mammoth machines clanging, lots of racket. Clatter, Clank, Creak.

Life expectancy plunging down due to child labour.

Factories flooding the streets of Great Britain,

People migrating to the city without second doubts.

Printing press carrying out mass productions, ink running out.

Machines being the new talk,

Massive workhouses taking up the city!

The world has changed in a flash.

I remember the machinery roaring, looking very dangerous to us.

Children getting deaf from the ear-piercing sounds.

 Engineers and factory workers running the city.

Locomotives – the main transport.

                                    Amelia, Humera, Mariah and Zarah

Bradford History

I remember the way everything was underdeveloped.

The history,

From first at foundation, to how things are today.

From working children, to a society of freedom,

Where children get an education.

Nellie and tramways still stand here today,

So here we stay,

Remembering the past.

From air full of combustion,

To clear and crisp skies.

Horsepower, locomotive, chassis, engineer,

This is what makes the car of the past.

This is the history of Bradford.

Hasna, Laila, Areesha and Ameerah

I Remember, I Remember, I Remember

I remember the loom spinning as the clock was ticking….

It was loud with everyone running around.

I remember the ink pressing while everybody was

stressing.

Although, this could be wrong – their hope was very strong.

I remember the turbine turning as the small children were learning.

They were so confused but they were still very amused.

I remember the museum being diverse like the big universe.

It had a variety of things that made the museum bling.

I remember the set of equipment getting ready to go for shipment.

There were chisels and trains that roared at us like lions.

Saffiyah, Maliyah, Sara , Sarah and Aqsa

What I Remember

I remember the walls full of diverse

patterns of grief circling around my mind.

Pieces of yarn and cotton.

The typesetting of the ink – more glamorous than the colour pink.

Chassis of ancient cars made me want to travel to Mars.

The spinning turbine, the forged metal, the combustion of Nellie

Makes me want to watch it on telly.

Spinning spindles and tremendous tools.

The wool and loom can come in useful for the socks.

This is what I remember.

Alina, Sameya, Muqaddas and Yenawu

Bradford Industrial Museum

Arriving at the museum,

Heavy machinery emitting a burning smell,

One that makes me think of child labour.

Printing processers, stamps, type settings too,

Nellie the steam engine who transported waste.

I remember walking into the Industrial Museum,

Full of historical wonders,

The smell of smoke filled my lungs.

Up we go, first floor it is,

Where a giant coat with diverse patterns lay upon it.

The fumes of combustion wafted in the air,

They sway in the breeze as they cast upon the street following the path,

Further into the past Nellie the steam engine working in despair,

This is definitely not fair.

                    Ayesha , Khadija , and Yussayrah

CARLTON BOLLING - BRADFORD

Do You Know How It Feels?

Do you know how it feels?

یے؟ ہوتا محسوس کیسا یہ کہ ہیں جانتے آپ کیا

To be isolated,

Separated from everyone else,

Discriminated against just because of who you are?

ہیں۔ کون آپ کہ یے جاتا کیا سلوک امتیازی سے وجہ اس صرف

Do you know how it feels?

یے؟ ہوتا محسوس کیسا یہ کہ ہیں جانتے آپ کیا

To be scared for the safety of your own life,

To watch innocent people die right before you,

To have sleepless nights as you don't want to live reality?

چاہتے نہیں رہنا میں حقیقت آپ کیونکہ گزارنا راتیں خواب یے

Do you know how it feels?

یے؟ ہوتا محسوس کیسا یہ کہ ہیں جانتے آپ کیا

To watch your family being dragged away,

Not knowing what dangers wait for you around the corner,

To go through all that heartache and pain?

گزرنا۔ سے درد اور دکھ سارے اس

Do you know how it feels?

یے؟ ہوتا محسوس کیسا یہ کہ ہیں جانتے آپ کیا

To be deprived of food,

To have no access to clean water,

Only because of your past?

سے۔ وجہ کی ماضی اپنے صرف

Do you know how it feels?

یے؟ ہوتا محسوس کیسا یہ کہ ہیں جانتے آپ کیا

To be called a terrorist,

Rumours being spread about you,

When you were the first victims of terrorism?

تھے۔ ہوئے شکار پہلا کا گردی دہشت آپ جب

Do you know how it feels?...

یے؟ ہوتا محسوس کیسا یہ کہ ہیں جانتے آپ کیا

Do you know how it feels to be a Palestinian?

یے؟ لگتا کیسا ہونا فلسطینی کہ ہیں جانتے آپ کیا

Safaa

In the Middle of Englistan There's a Town Called Bradford

In the middle of Englistan there's a town called Bradford,

And to me it's not mud,

You'll see every good,

But the people are soft as bud,

Barkerend, Undercliffe and Idle have a new trend,

Cause we're good at making friends,

Where all Indians and Pakisitanis relations mend,

Bowlers like Adil Rashid,

Giving us two times the speed,

Muslims, Hindus and Christians follow their creed,

Always makin' sure they're doing the good deeds,

Yeh this is Bradford we're talkin' about,

And yeh you can't take its spirit out,

Mosques, temples and churches they pray,

Can't stop prayin' till their hair's gray,

Yay hai Bradford dosato,

If you wanna learn more *to aja close ho,*

Yahaa miltay hay behtareen masalay,

Tumhe book ho to ajaa ka lay,

Yahi miltay zaberdast roti,

Aur agar curry kanay ho to ajayay kahlo Akbar's curry,

Chicken ke malik to Salah hi hai,

Fish ke rani Mother Hubbard's hai,

Yo lads now you've had a taste of us,

Don't go back to Nottingham in a bus,

As you know here there is every good,

So in the middle of Englistan there's a town called Bradford.

Umaiz

Salam Alaikum

Salam alaikum is the way to greet

this is the way we meet

From the youngest to the eldest

Salam alaikum is the way to greet

Hum Salam alakikum kei sath suro karthe hamari baat

Khushi ki baat ho yah aur udass ki baat ho

Hum Salam alakikum kei sath suro karthe hamari baat

They laugh and mock our mother tongue

Teaching us to hide our identity from when we were young

Salam alaikum

But our souls are enlightened when we witness another soul greet us

with *Salam alaikum*

The hate of the world vanishes from our shoulder when they speak their

mother tongue.

Aroosh and Tasnim

Society

I hear people saying
'all lives matter
We are all the same'
Now I think that's wrong
but you're not to blame
All lives do matter
but you're not going to get equality on a silver platter

You have to fight for it
strive for it
and one day
you'll achieve it
I'm not here to discourage you
but to correct you

We are not all the same
It's for that very reason humans thrive
and survive
If we're all the same
then we have identical stories
identical lives

But life is much more diverse than that
individual lives, planets, universes

We cross paths
Feel the same

Bet atcerieties, ka mēs visi esam atšķirīgi, ne visi vienādi
Es varu runāt latviski
Jūs varētu runāt franču vai vācu valodā.

So rethink your ideas
and think about this:
Be true to yourself
Everyone's different
All lives are important
that's no lie
But when it comes to being yourself
you shouldn't be shy
Your life is your story
not somebody else's
Make your story unique
Something nobody's done
Because at the end of the day
the point of life is to have fun.

Yet we squabble
and fight
in the darkness
for light
Though as we keep fighting

the light fades

We fight even more

with our guns and our blades

Hope fading

Humans degrading

Society collapsing

Differences elapsing

We fight for race, culture and land

It's time we took a stand

because standing together is

better than standing

alone

The earth is our home

we must cherish it, nurture it

Do whatever it takes

yet we are blind to the violence it makes

Now I'm a foreigner and

don't quite know how this country works

But something is going wrong

Disaster after disaster after disaster

We try to keep things normal yet

What do we do?

We fight

and fight

and fight

This, is humans' fatal flaw

the day that the crows will caw

is the day we destroy the earth

with our violence and war

It's in our nature, we're violent and reckless

however when the crows caw no longer

we realise that our violence and war

has made our home no more.

Niks

A United World

The world is broken, fragmented like shattered glass
Torn down by words spoken about social status and class.

We call for justice, but the damage is already done
A problem rooted in our past, a topic we mustn't shun.

Don't make the mistake of thinking that it can be solved overnight
Discrimination is still a problem many people are having to fight.

Why do our differences determine the way we are treated?
Making some feel inferior and others conceited.

Despite the rules and laws, you only point out our flaws
You ignore the value we add, all you see is the bad.

Let's stop the divide and conquer, you know it's not right
We need to make things better, we need to unite.

So let us respect each other and create a world where we all fit in
A world where we set aside our differences, a world where we all win.

Priya

War

I'm trying to get a new high score,

How many people will I kill today?

قف

[Stop]

الأبرياء؟ لقتل عليه السيطرة يمكن لا الذي دافعك ، ماذا توقف

[Stop what, your uncontrollable urge to murder innocents?]

I am messing with the lives of our brave, unaware soldiers.

What if they don't come back from the battlefield?

At least we'll be safe knowing that our country is not a target.

الحرب هذه في ننتصر أن حقًا آمل

[I really hope we win this war]

Remember when we used to care about everyone,

No matter who they were or where they came from?

I miss them times.

ضعفاء كنا

[We were weak]

We tried to make our community a better place!

One day, we had just finished cleaning up the park,

Then we saw the poster...

'The tragedy of war is that it uses man's best to do man's worst.'

HOW AM I IN THIS POSITION OF MILITARY LEADER??

.لبلده شيء أي سيفعل الإرادة قوي محارب أنت

[You are a strong-willed warrior who would do anything for his country]

Would I?

There must be another solution to this problem.

If only you understood -

Understood that cities and ethnicities would be destroyed?

Generations upon generations murdered?

الرهيب الغزو هذا أوقفوا

[Stop this horrible invasion]

.الحديث نهاية ، جنودنا نشرنا

[We've deployed our soldiers, end of conversation]

Ibraheem

1 Life, 1 Gone, 1 Time No More

First light it began

one beginning that has no end

eyes open at the anticipation of new sight

as they get accepted by families' cry of excitement

the cry of the baby is born

The next bairn to resume a families' legacy

Will become the new hope again

The journey has just begun

That lifetime ahead is now decades of work

As the new doors become wide open

The world now at the doorstep

Now it was easy, nae, it took steps before the walking for the walking to become the running

Oh the running, where it would carry us to unknown places

And with a wee bit more time, we can run outdoors -

To an open field where you only see sunlight, never full moons

While the rays, they hide unknown shadows to you

Soon you will know why (one day they say, one day)

Over time, few words changed to full sentences

Silent murmurs once heard blossoms into questions spoken of by you

But really there is only one question to be had

'What is beyond there?'

Past walls made to confine you, past ceilings that block out something above you

Whatever it is, you will find out as quick as possible

You will be unaware of the dangers to come

It is alright, the adventure is part of what creates the fun

Quickly you follow the path that had begun to sprout

Seeing one's face filled with glee the closer you get

While your childish laughter begins to be heard

From youthful energy bursting out as if their minds are going to pop

But before you set to embark on your new path, one decayed, old person is seen

Solemn and silent, still and sorrowful, only staring in one direction

They seem lost when they are surrounded by the world

The world of family, discovery and wee bit of love

Instead, they are accepting something, but what?

Who cares? Why wait for the night when the sun is still out?

It is just 1 elderly person

One step outside and the world opens up to them

with the breeze of the wind sliding past your cheek

you are urged to take another step, just to feel the mud squelch
beneath your feet

one foot dirty now, here is the other

brown coloured mud, stains your shoes but you do not care

you see straight lines of fields as high as you

looks like a maze if you get lost but still you venture forward

the deeper you go, you notice white, fluffy objects floating on a blue
canvas

look as soft as your old pillar back in yer bed

1 sky seen by 1 you

higher and higher you look to feel warmth on yer face

just to draw back from the light it bestows

it feels powerful, but still warm like the blanket of yer bed

as even if it was never your home, it is a place you can call it home

that 1 true home

alas, no place can retain their permanence

soon, rays of sunlight fade

and a scary monster comes out thou has been told

you dash back to sweet mother holding the door open

back to familiar walls and ceilings to hide behind

Time takes their toll, causing decades to years

a once innocent, young mind now a broken wretch

even exquisite sentences are all but puzzled words

with potential opportunities feeling like hapless failures

and when you take a step outside, it remains a rotting mess

where fields once lay become bumpy holes

alongside wilting weeds replace a once lush land...

of darkened clouds confused and lost

the sun is no longer at thy peak

so, whatever it is you uncovered

it is no longer what you want it to be

the 1 place thought to never change, no more

confused smiles and frowns only describe you

and while trudging home, the door… closed

you push, tug and bang still the blasted thing won't open

using every strength, you crash at the door, just for it to barely open

looks like even the hinges are beginning to age

Eventually, years changed to months

The broken you finally patches one's self together

sparking old passions once started, never finished

relighting old you back to glory, maybe

re-aligning the path to the set course

so, you can finally set sail smoothly

prepare for life to slam their door

only this time, you're ready for the world and embark once more

You take a step to… nothing

1 destroyed land of decayed matter

where grasslands use to stay, are now ravaged with pot holes and hills too hard to climb

1 bleak sky

how it hosts hazy, black mist rather than endless white clouds

1 full moon shining its dim light

replacing the sun that used to guide us on the very path that started it all

the only answer is to run, not forward, away from this hell hole

as it is up to you

to escape from these shadows taking over you

you run fast, just for the door to be shut again

only this time, there is no point in banging, as you're locked out of yer safe house

locked out from parents that used to shield you from those shadows

you are on your own

to re-open the door

many attempts it took, but somehow it opens for you to stumble in

Months are now only days

every burden stacks upon another

'These old bones cannot move anymore'

while the black turns into greys

silence and sorrow is your only cure

since you will fall

when time reaches zero

devils and angels will be seeing to your fate, they say

one shed tear may be the last, no longer you can say

'You can change that'

no longer you can say that you can

'Rise back up'

When you reach the end of the journey

You hear a child, so curious and happy

Starting the beginning of their legacy

And you, reaching the end of your legacy

Past life experiences ahead

Rabeh

UNIVERSITY ACADEMY KEIGHLEY

- BRADFORD

A Place I Want to Leave

A place I want to leave
Yet a place where I belong
A place where everyone's more experienced than you
And everyone's telling you you're wrong.

Lots of taunts from my siblings
But that just toughens you up.
'Cos the world's got harsher people out there
And the house is tough enough.

My home is the tinted windows
My home is doing what you're told
My home is a constant noise in my ears
And the noisier neighbours across the road.

My home is a web of lies and secrets
My home is where you laugh yourself sore
My home is where people slam the door in your face
But they always open some more.

Huda

Brother

You were the conversations shared at night so long that my hands pruned while washing the dishes.

The two pillows beneath my head after my ejection from the sofa, being forced to sit on the carpet.

The plots of shows I've never seen told within the confines of the kitchen that bled into my dreams.

You were the omnipresent figure in my life

when people came and left.

The incessant voice that yelled 'close the door' like clockwork

The insults hurled that never ceased, even when comforting me.

You were the emptiness that was only filled at your return home,

The words commented when watching a movie, which hung heavy in the air

As I stared at an empty living room.

The white lies told which pushed me into panic, feeling no remorse at our mother's reprimanding.

You were frustration and annoyance

My elation and sorrow.

To me, you were my home.

Tina

To My Home

The peace of my life will always be connected to you

You were with me from the day I took my first breath

To my last.

Even if I move away one step, a mile or more

You'll always be there.

Because it isn't the four walls I connect with

It's the people inside.

To my mum

Who braided my hair as a child

And my dad

Who taught me to be a strong young woman

And my siblings

Who made me realise anger is okay.

They'll always be my home.

                                                             Imaan

Home

A kitchen always smelling of curry

Mum always hassling and cooking

A living room filled with cousins and siblings

Watching movies all day.

The scary cellar

that no-one enters.

My bedroom door always closed

And the guest room always open.

My room is filled with clothes on clothes

And the other rooms are surrounded with toys

My baby brother trying to climb the stairs

And my dad coming back from work.

I've lost the TV remote, chargers and toys

Mum complaining that I'm on my phone

And siblings always yelling.

The living room is dark purple with gold embellishments

And the kitchen is shades of grey.

My room is where I feel safe, my cosy bed, bright LED lights

And a drawer crammed with sweets.

This is home.

Saima

BRADFORD GIRLS GRAMMAR

SCHOOL-BRADFORD

As soon as...

As soon as I close my eyes
the smell of salty, fish water from the river rushes
 towards me along with the voices of people happily chatting
 con la música classical played in the background,
I feel the cold breeze bumping into my skin giving me goosebumps,
I smell the flowers and the fresh air
As I remember, in childhood, playing with my best friends
 beneath the pine tree surrounded by many flowers.
I miss sitting on the bench, eating the gelado de chocolate
, surrounded by my friends.

From a baby born in Pakistan
To a little girl playing Em Centro de Tavira,
To a twelve year old walking down a hill in Bradford,
going home.

                                                      Ruwaeda

Howarth

From the wind to the trees

Through the buzzing of the bees I finally reached

Where I had been in my dreams Although I have been there only once

I feel like going there every month

The place was marvelous that it took my heart

From the hills to the graveyard to the museum everything seemed to

pyaree

The smell of fish and chips made bhooka but I could not waste my time

eating because I knew there was more to come

Staying and exploring made me forget about home I replaced it with

somewhere pretty but unknown

People in the graveyard made me think about how many difficulties

they had to overcome which made them our role models as they also

showed us the straight path to a better future

Maryam

Memories

From loud roads to noisy streams,

From postcard pretty hills to mountains covered with clouds, Skies full

of stars, moonlight of a thousand watts,

Reservoirs canals rivers with rushing streams and waterfalls,

Mossy rocks to mighty oaks,

Landscapes and flowers not just pretty to look at but worthy to be

painted,

Dandelions dancing with the wind, ready to land,

From bees buzzing to birds chirping all together cherishing a world,

A place that one could only cherish in their dream,

A place that may be unknown to many,

A place unknown to the map,

Yet a place that brings back Memories.

Zara

Around Yorkshire from LS8 to BD9

From LS8 to BD9

From squished terraced houses

To spacious semi detached

From roti and keer to enchillades and banofee pie

First Bagjees park and now Lister

From chai to hot chocolate

Streets covered with happy children

Roads covered with litter

LS8 filled with rows of shops

I left Leeds and came to Bradford

Lister park, Chellow dean, canals, rivers,

Rushing streams and waterfalls.

Pink and white blossoms, antique made of stone mills

Emerald fields and mighty oaks

Eye watering air, blinding sun

Luxurious landscapes

Both are beautiful places with ups and downs

As well as unique differences

My Place Pakistan

My heart's beating jaldi

Dog's barking and running

Cows drinking and eating

Turtles swimming and splashing

What a hot day!

My mouth is tasting the kulfi that made of milk

It's the flowers that I can smell

But never take me away from Pakistan

What can I do, It's the animals that annoy

Pictures coming in my mind

Feel like sleeping

But I'm eating

Dhai palle, Biryani, Pakore, Samose, fruit chart, chawal for dinner

Dhai and Pudna for chutney

Guava and doodh for milkshake

Wow! What's like Pakistani food

Oh! You know I'm a Pakistani girl

Busy cleaning up, Busy watching Kahaniya

Busy shopping, Busy reading, Busy dreaming

Sitting in riksha and going to bazar, auntie's house, mamu's house

On the rocky roads had llots of jumps

On the travel, in the forms, on the hills

I saw bakria, horses and donkeys

Went to the sea and saw lots of machlia

I'm a Pakistani girl

Eshaal

Printed in Great Britain
by Amazon